Magic, Myth, and Mystery

DWARFS

DO YOU BELIEVE?

This series features creatures that excite our minds. They're magical. They're mythical. They're mysterious. They're also not real. They live in our stories. They're brought to life by our imaginations. Facts about these creatures are based on folklore, legends, and beliefs. We have a rich history of believing in the impossible. But these creatures only live in fantasies and dreams. Monsters do not live under our beds. They live in our heads!

45th Parallel Press

Published in the United States of America by Cherry Lake Publishing
Ann Arbor, Michigan
www.cherrylakepublishing.com

Reading Adviser: Marla Conn MS, Ed., Literacy specialist, Read-Ability, Inc.
Book Design: Felicia Macheske

Photo Credits: © © Fernando Cortes//Shutterstock.com, cover; © Potapov Alexander/Shutterstock.com;
© LaKirr/Shutterstock.com, 1; © Drpixel/Shutterstock.com, 5; © rangizzz/Shutterstock.com, 7; © wjarek/
Shutterstock.com, 8; © Dmitrijs Bindemanis/Shutterstock.com, 11; © Captblack76/Shutterstock.com, 12;
© Sergio Foto/Shutterstock.com, 15; © mrmohock/Shutterstock.com, 17; © Nomad_Soul/Shutterstock.com, 18;
© Vladimir Kant/Shutterstock.com, 20; © Pecold/Shutterstock.com, 23; © TTstudio/Shutterstock.com, 24;
© Maria Starovoytova/Shutterstock.com, 27; © Holger Kirk/Shutterstock.com, 27; © SERGEI BALDIN/
Shutterstock.com, 29

Graphic Elements Throughout: © denniro/Shutterstock.com; © Libellule/Shutterstock.com; © sociologas/
Shutterstock.com; © paprika/Shutterstock.com; © ilolab/Shutterstock.com; © Bruce Rolff/Shutterstock.com

45th Parallel Press is an imprint of Cherry Lake Publishing.

Library of Congress Cataloging-in-Publication Data has been filed and is available at catalog.loc.gov

Cherry Lake Publishing would like to acknowledge the work of The Partnership for 21st Century Skills.
Please visit *www.p21.org* for more information.

Printed in the United States of America
Corporate Graphics Inc.

TABLE of CONTENTS

Minds Made for Mining

What are dwarfs? What do they do? What do they look like?

"Heigh-ho! Heigh-ho! It's off to work we go!" Dwarfs are hard workers. They're **miners**. Miners dig into the earth. They chip into rock. They find gems. But dwarfs do other jobs. They do **smithing**. Smithing means working with metal. They make weapons. They make supplies. They're experts with their hands. They're very smart.

They live in mountains. They dig through rock. They dig caves and tunnels. They also live underground. They dig down deep. They dig underground mazes.

They spend most of their time mining. They collect gold, silver, and other stones. They save their treasures in caves.

Dwarfs are the engineers of the monster world.

Explained by Science!

Dwarfism is a medical condition. It refers to having a short build. People with dwarfism are usually shorter than 4 feet (1.2 meters). Some people with dwarfism have the same size body parts. Some people with dwarfism have shorter body parts. Dwarfism can be caused by abnormal bone growth. Achondroplasia is the most common form of dwarfism. It starts at birth. About one in 30,000 babies has it. They may suffer some health problems. But people with dwarfism are smart. They have formed groups. They want to help each other. Science has also created helpful tools for people with dwarfism. They have cars, clothing, furniture, and medical tools they are able to use. Some dogs have achondroplasia. They have short legs. Examples are dachshunds, basset hounds, corgis, and bulldogs.

They live in groups. Each group has its own leader. Each group also has its own army. Dwarfs live together. They work together. They live for hundreds of years. There are more male dwarfs than females.

They look like humans. But they're shorter. They're about 3 feet (1 meters) tall. They're stocky. They have a lot of muscles. They're ugly. They have big heads. They have big hands. They have big feet. They have humped backs. They have pale skin. They look old. They're hairy. Their hair is white. Males have long beards.

Dwarfs are also called Earth-Men.

Dwarfs are from the **fairy** family. They're a type of fairy. Fairies are magical creatures. They're spirits. They're **supernatural**. They're beyond the laws of nature.

There are different types of dwarfs. White dwarfs are peaceful. They're kind. They make art from gold and silver. Brown dwarfs make trouble. They steal babies. They cause **nightmares**. They play tricks on people. Black dwarfs are evil. They make deadly weapons. They set up fake lights. They crash ships into rocks. Red dwarfs are dangerous. They cause fights. They're **omens**. Omens are signs of bad things to come.

Dwarfs usually wear hats.

Chapter Two

Magical Weapon Makers

What magic do dwarfs have? What are some of the weapons they make?

Dwarfs have secret knowledge. They have great wisdom. They know things. They have the power to see the future.

They have magical powers. They can make people sick. They can give people warts. They can heal people. Some dwarfs can make themselves **invisible**. Invisible means not able to be seen. Some dwarfs can change their shapes.

Dwarfs are good fighters. They defend their homes. They defend their treasures. They like to use axes. But they use all kinds of weapons. They make the best weapons. They make very **innovative** weapons. Innovative means modern and creative.

Dwarfs have magic but don't use it unless they have to.

Dwarfs make other powerful items. They make jewelry. They make charms. They add magic. They give these items to gods. They're special gifts.

Dwarfs made Tyrfing. This was a magical sword. The sword could fight by itself. It never missed. It never rusted. It was sharp. But dwarfs weren't happy. They were forced to work. So, they **cursed** the sword. Curses are magical spells that make bad things happen. They cursed it to kill someone every time it was used. They cursed it to cause three great evils. They cursed it to kill a king.

Sometimes, dwarfs are tricked to make magical weapons.

When Fantasy Meets Reality!

Nematode worms were found in mines. They were found far beneath Earth's surface. Living things usually can't live at this level. It's too hot to sustain life. There's no sunlight. There's little oxygen. There's no food. But nematode worms found a way. They're really tiny. They're tubes that eat and poop. They live in water squeezed between the rocks. They feed off bacteria. They can live in hot weather. They've been living there for 3,000 to 12,000 years. This means they evolved over time. They changed to live through high pressures and high heats. Scientists are happy about this discovery. This means that there's a chance there could be life on Mars and other planets. These worms have been called the devil worm. They've also been called worms from hell.

Some of the dwarfs' weapons have names.

Dwarfs made Thor's hammer. Thor was the god of thunder. This hammer crushed everything it was aimed at. It never missed. It could find its way back to the owner. It could change its size.

Dwarfs made Draupnir. This was a magical gold ring. Eight new rings would drop out of it. This happened every ninth day. All the rings were gold. This made the owner rich.

Dwarfs made a magical chain. It bound a powerful wolf. Dwarfs made a magical spear. It hit whatever it was thrown at. Dwarfs made a magical ship. It always sailed in good wind. It could be folded up. Dwarfs even made a head of hair.

Chapter Three

Naughty or Nice

How are dwarfs helpful? How are they harmful? How can they be stopped?

Dwarfs can be nice. They have a lot of skills. They're wise. They take pride in their work. They do kind things. They find lost animals. They put out food. They feed poor children. They repay the people who help them. They give them some of their treasures.

But they can also be mean. They're stubborn. They don't forget or forgive. They hold grudges. They steal food. They tease farm animals. They steal children. They punish people who steal their treasures. They turn the treasures into dead leaves. They curse robbers.

Dwarfs respect age, wealth, and talent.

Dwarfs are mysterious.

Dwarfs hate **elves**. Elves are also a type of fairy. They're the opposite of dwarfs. Some elves are tiny. Some are tall. They have pointy ears. They have great beauty. They look young.

Dwarfs don't trust them. Elves have raided their homes. They've stolen their riches. Dwarfs and elves have been in many wars. Dwarfs don't always win. They're good fighters. But they're slow runners. They're poor riders.

Dwarfs avoid humans. They don't speak human languages. They like to test humans. Some humans don't treat dwarfs well. So, dwarfs get even. They plan tricks. They curse things.

SURVIVAL TIPS!

- Wait for morning. Lead dwarfs out to the sun. Dwarfs turn to stone in the sun.

- Wear iron. Fairies don't like iron. Since dwarfs are fairies, this may annoy them.

- Avoid mountains and going underground. Dwarfs might live there.

- Don't steal dwarfs' treasures. Stay away from their stuff. Dwarfs don't like to be robbed.

- Don't make dwarfs mad. Don't play tricks on them. Dwarfs like to get even. They don't mess around. They go after their enemies.

Dwarfs live in dark, tight spaces. They've become night creatures. They can see in the dark. They live on less air. They move slowly to save energy. Some dwarfs are known as night demons. They cause sleeping problems. They cause nightmares. Nightmares are scary dreams.

Dwarfs don't see the sun much. In fact, they don't like the sun. The sun can kill them. If sunlight hits them, they can turn to stone. People thought **megaliths** were dwarfs. Megaliths are big standing stones. They look like stone people.

Some people think dwarfs may be spirits of the dead.

Chapter Four

Stones and Stories

When did dwarfs start showing up in history? How did dwarf stories start?

Dwarfs were around when Stonehenge was being built. Stonehenge is a megalith. Stonehenge is a ring of standing stones. It's in an open field.

Ancient people took about 1,500 years to build Stonehenge. It was built between 3,000 BCE and 1,600 BCE. It was finished in the **Bronze Age**. The Bronze Age was an early period in human history. It was when people made tools from **bronze**. Bronze is a mixture of copper and tin.

Stonehenge is located in Wiltshire, England.

There were tin miners in the Bronze Age. These miners were from southern Europe. Southern people were short. They had beards. They knew a lot about mining. They knew a lot about metal. They made weapons.

But tin was running out. So, the southern miners moved to the north. There was more tin there. They showed the northern people how to mine. They showed them how to make things out of metal. Mining looked like magic. This may be how stories about dwarfs started.

Dwarfs are connected with stones and mining.

Know the Lingo!

- **Andvari:** a dwarf who owns treasure stolen by the Norse trickster god named Loki

- **Blainn:** limbs of the dead; used to create dwarfs

- **Brimir:** blood of fire; used to create dwarfs

- **Duergar:** evil race of dwarfs from *Dungeons and Dragons*

- **Dvergr:** old Norse word for dwarfs

- **Dwergh:** old English word for dwarfs

- **Krasnale:** Polish word for dwarfs

- **Nibelung:** a dwarf who owns treasure stolen by the Norse hero named Siegfried

- **Roarie:** leader of the Simonside Dwarfs

- **Simonside Dwarfs:** a race of ugly dwarfs from the northern England area around Simonside Hills

- **Tolkien Dwarves:** dwarfs created by J.R.R. Tolkien

- **Wio Dweorh:** a charm meaning "against a dwarf" used to help people sleep

Chapter Five

Beyond the Seven Dwarfs

What are some stories about dwarfs?

Dwarfs are also in **Norse myths**. Norse means coming from an area around Norway. Myths are stories.

Odin is a Norse god. He fought against Ymir. Ymir is a giant. Odin killed Ymir. **Maggots** came out of Ymir's body. Maggots are the worm stages of a fly's life. Ymir's maggots dug through his body. Odin gave the maggots a human form. But they kept digging through earth and rock. They became dwarfs.

Odin gave four dwarfs a special job. The four dwarfs are Austri, Vestri, Norori, and Suori. This means East, West, North, and South. Their job was to hold up the sky. The sky was created from Ymir's **skull**. Skulls are bones of heads.

Norse dwarfs were made of blood and bones.

Real-World Connection

Wroclaw's dwarfs are small statues. They're bronze. They're about a foot tall. They first showed up in 2005. They cover the streets of Wroclaw, Poland. They're all over the city. They've become very popular. There are over 400 dwarfs. People go "hunting" for these dwarfs. They get special maps. The city hosts a yearly Great Dwarf Parade. People dress up the dwarfs. The dwarfs are in honor of the Orange Alternative. The Orange Alternative was an anti-Soviet movement. Its symbol was a dwarf. A member said, "The dwarves gave us something to laugh at." Tomasz Moczek is an artist. He had an idea. He made dwarfs and put them around the city. The first dwarf was placed where the group met. It was named Papa Dwarf. Moczek has created over 100 dwarfs. This inspired other artists to create dwarfs, too.

Dwarfs are also common in German myths. The most famous German dwarfs are Snow White's seven dwarfs. They helped Snow White escape from her evil stepmother.

Biloko are part of central African stories. They're dwarfs. They have no hair. They have sharp claws. They have sharp teeth. They live in the forests. They guard the forests. They're the spirits of dead family members. They're unhappy. They haunt the living. They swallow humans whole. They put magical spells on humans.

Kuei Xing is from Chinese stories. He's a smart, ugly dwarf. He's the god of tests.

German dwarfs healed and mined.

Did You Know?

- One dwarf is spelled "dwarf." More than one dwarf is spelled "dwarfs." But it can also be spelled "dwarves." "Dwarfs" is more commonly used. J.R.R. Tolkien made "dwarves" popular. He's a famous writer. He wrote *The Hobbit* and *The Lord of the Rings*. But he admitted "dwarves" was a mistake. He said, "I am afraid it is just a piece of private bad grammar...but I shall have to go with it."

- The word *dwarf* comes from a root word meaning "to deceive." In German stories, dwarfs play tricks.

- The "seven dwarfs" are real. The Ovitz family were Romanian Jews. Simson Ovitz was a dwarf. He had 10 children. Seven of the children were dwarfs. They're the largest family of dwarfs. They're the largest family to survive Auschwitz. The children formed a musical group. They called themselves the Lilliput Troupe. They performed all over Europe.

- The Mayans had a myth about a dwarf. A dwarf passed three tests. First, he became king. Then he built a palace. Then he built a city. The city's buildings were part of the Uxmal ruins.

- There's an urban legend in Wisconsin. The Haunchies of Muskego are dwarfs. They live on Mystic Road. They may have been former circus workers. They lived in small houses. They built underground tunnels to escape. They don't like people coming to their town. If people get too close, they attack. They cut people at the knees to make them short. They beat up people. They hang them from a tree. They set them on fire.